LEVEL 2

Saturday Storm

Julia Newsome

Richmond READERS

◪ **Richmond** READERS

LEVEL 1

(500 headwords)

Maria's Dilemma
Oscar
Jack's Game
The Boy from Yesterday
The Black Mountain

LEVEL 2

(800 headwords)

Jason Causes Chaos
Craigen Castle Mystery
The Road through the Hills and othes stories
Where's Mauriac?
Saturday Storm

LEVEL 3

(1200 headwords)

A Trip to the Stars
Dr Jekyll and Mr Hyde
The Canterville Ghost and Other Stories
Cold Feet
Frankenstein

LEVEL 4

(1800 headwords)

A Trip to London
Dracula
Jane Eyre
The Adventures of Tom Sawyer
Sense and Sensibility

LEVEL 5

(2600+ headwords)

Steve Jobs: the man behind Apple
Elizabeth II The Diamond Queen

Saturday Storm

Philip thinks everyone is against him – his father does not understand him, his mother does not care about him, his sister argues with him, his brother is too young. Tension builds up.

The family set off for Philip's basketball match on Saturday morning. A storm builds up in the sky. They hear a distant roll of thunder*...

....

Julia Newsome taught English to adults at work and children at school for twenty years in Athens, Greece. She now lives half the time in Belgium and the other half in England, but she often visits Greece. She teaches English and writes stories and teaching books. She likes going to the cinema and walking in the country. Julia has two children.

LEVEL 2

CHARACTERS IN THE STORY

Jim and Penny Alexiou
*Philip's father and mother; Jim is a history and music
teacher, Penny is a pharmacist.*

*Philip Alexiou age 17,
plays basketball and
computer games, in his
last year at school*

*Viki Alexiou
age 16, plays
basketball*

*Alex Alexiou
age 7*

*Harris Levendis
owner of a computer shop*

*Steve and Chris
Philip's friends and members
of basketball team*

*Luke Makris
Basketball team* trainer**

*Barbara
Viki's friend and Philip's girlfriend*

4

CHAPTER 1

Sunday: lunch

'Your score*,' the computer said, 'is three thousand, one hundred and fifty. This is the highest score ever.'

'Of course it is,' Philip said to his computer. 'I can play this game in my sleep. I've played it thousands of times. I need some new games...'

'Philip! Lunch!' His mother always called Philip first. That gave him time to turn off the computer. Then she called his father. 'Jim, Jim!' Then his father answered, 'Coming, Penny.' It was always the same.

His mother called again. 'Viki, Alex, where are you? Lunch time.' Sundays never changed. The computer screen went black.

The smell of cooked meat came from the kitchen. Viki was already there, alone.

'Viki should cut all that hair,' Philip thought. 'Then people could believe she's sixteen and not ten.' She was taking a piece of tomato from the big salad bowl in the middle of the table.

He wanted to surprise her.

'I saw you,' he said loudly.

'Mm...,' she said with her mouth full. 'It's nice.' She smiled. 'Try some. It's good for you.'

'I hate tomato,' Philip said. He sat down in his usual place at the table.

Viki sat opposite him.

The computer screen went black.

'You hate most things these days,' she said sadly.

Their little brother, Alex, came running into the kitchen. He was carrying a plant with pink flowers. He was very dirty.

'I got this from the field,' he said. 'It's for Grandma.'

'Oh Alex, you look terrible,' Viki said. 'Wash your hands and face. Now!'

'OK, OK,' Alex said. He put the plant by the window.

Their father came in.

'Here, I'll help you,' he said, and father and son washed together. They laughed as the water went everywhere. Philip sat with his back to them.

Penny came in from the garden with two lemons in her hand.

'That's enough!' she said. 'Sit down quietly, everyone. Philip, could you cut these lemons, please?'

They all sat down at the table and began to eat and pass things to each other. There was quiet for a few moments.

'Jim,' Penny said. 'Have you seen Alex's shoes? They're full of holes. We must get him a new pair.'

'More shoes?' Jim asked. He was surprised.

'More.' Penny said sadly. 'Philip last week, Alex this week.'

'Oh, and Dad,' Viki said. 'I need new basketball boots for our match* on Wednesday.'

Jim looked at his daughter.

'Of course, of course,' he said, and he smiled. 'And

new shoes and a new dress for the disco tonight...'

'And a new coat and a new bag to go with them,' Viki said. She was laughing. 'Poor Dad.'

'Seriously, Dad,' Philip said. 'There is something I need. All the computer games I've got are too easy for me now. There's a new program that helps you to write computer games yourself. It's expensive, but you learn a lot and you can write twenty games or more ... Please, Dad?'

Jim looked down at his food for a few moments. Finally he said, 'You have a basketball match, too, don't you? On Saturday?'

Philip went red. 'Yes,' he said. 'It's away*, against the Mountain Villagers.'

'Luke Makris, your new trainer, has asked me and some other parents* to come with you,' Jim said.

'Yeah*!' Alex said loudly. 'We'll show them who's best.'

'All the family can come and support* the team,' said Jim. Penny looked at Jim. 'Except Mum, of course,' he said. 'She's busy on Saturday.'

'Oh, Mum,' Philip said. 'Please come!'

'Not this time, love,' Penny said with a smile. 'I have to help Grandma with something.'

Philip suddenly felt very angry. Why was Grandma more important than he was?

'It doesn't matter,' he said in a hard voice. 'I'm sure Viki will find someone to bring with her. How about that strange guy* you're meeting at the disco tonight,

* *Colloquial form of 'Yes'*

Viki? What's his name? Ted? Or maybe Johnny, the English teacher's son, or Mark from the music shop... I know! You could come in Mark's car, so Dad could bring Mum *and* Grandma.'

'Oh, Philip, be serious,' Viki said. 'The boys we meet at the disco are really boring. They're only interested in loud music and stupid clothes. The boys I like are in your team. But they're always busy training* and they never go to the disco.'

Viki was smiling and eating chips with her fingers. Philip had stopped eating and now he sat without moving. He was looking at Viki. His face was dark and angry.

Jim said quietly, 'Viki, don't eat with your fingers.' He turned to Philip. 'I told Luke that we could come. The other two families are going on Friday afternoon, but we can follow the team in the minibus* on Saturday morning.' He looked along the table to Penny. 'What else have you got for us to eat, my love?'

'Fruit salad and ice-cream,' answered Penny. 'That's your favourite, Philip.'

'I don't care if you give us ice-cream for breakfast, lunch and dinner!' Philip shouted*. He stood up. His chair fell to the floor. 'You seem to think I'm still a baby like Alex!'

'Hey!' Alex started to speak, but Philip did not hear him.

'You forget that other things are important to me, Mum. I want all my family there to watch the match,

Viki was smiling and eating chips with her fingers.

but you don't care. And you,' Philip turned to his father, his face red. Jim stood up slowly. 'You don't care that I want to be the best with computers. You don't care that I want to get a job using computers. That's why I have to learn a lot about them. Have you forgotten that I leave school in four months? You live in the past and you don't see how fast things are changing. You don't see that I could make a lot of money working with computers. Then I won't have to be old and poor like you!' Philip went out and shut the door with a bang*.

Jim sat down and put his face in his hands. Penny and Viki were silent.

Alex said, 'Can I have Phil's ice-cream?'

CHAPTER **2** (3)

Tuesday: after school

Viki and her friend, Barbara, came out of the school building. It was time to go home.

'Oh no!' Barbara said. 'It's raining and the school bus is late.'

They ran to the great tree that stood in front of the school. There were a lot of students under it, keeping out of* the rain. Philip was there with two of his friends, Chris and Steve. Viki got as close to Chris as she could. Then she and Barbara turned their backs.

They became very interested in Barbara's magazine. They were not listening, of course, but they could hear every word the boys said.

The boys were looking at Chris's mobile phone.

'It works anywhere in the country,' Chris said. 'And the battery lasts for ninety minutes of calls.'

'How much was it?' Philip asked.

'I don't know. It was a birthday present from my uncle,' Chris said.

'Some people have all the luck,' Philip said. 'None of *my* uncles is rich enough to give me birthday presents like that.'

'Nor mine,' Steve said, laughing. 'I get a "nice book" or a cassette if I'm lucky!'

'But your parents are rich!' Philip said. 'You moved into that big new house last year. And your cousin got a motorbike for his birthday.'

'My parents have no extra money *because* of the big new house,' Steve said. 'And my cousin works now. He's buying the motorbike himself with some of the money he makes each month.'

'It's a great bike,' Chris said. 'Have you seen how fast it goes? Over two hundred kilometres an hour!'

Viki could not stop herself. 'A real killing machine,' she said, turning round.

Steve turned to her. 'Not if you're careful. Luke has a big bike – you know Luke, the new basketball trainer?

The boys were looking at Chris's mobile phone.

He comes to training on it. He's always careful.'

'Most boys I know,' Barbara said in a loud voice, 'prefer going fast to being careful.'

No one spoke for a few moments. Chris and Philip turned away.

'Who are you playing against tomorrow?' Steve asked Viki.

'The Coast Schools,' Viki answered. 'They're a strong team but we're playing at home*, so there's a good chance we'll win.'

'Would you like ... er ... could ... er ... should we ..?' Steve's face went pink and he looked down.

'Sorry?' Barbara said. 'What did you say?'

'Nothing, nothing,' Steve said. He was looking for something in his school bag.

'Viki,' Philip said suddenly. 'You are, of course, the best girl basketball player in town. And perfect players don't need help ... But why don't I bring three or four friends to support you tomorrow night?'

'Oh, are you coming, then?' Viki asked, half smiling. 'I don't want to make life difficult for you, big brother. I'm sure we'll do fine without you.'

'No, listen, it'll be good,' Chris said. 'We'll support you tomorrow and you can support us on Saturday.'

'Are you coming on Saturday, Viki?' Steve asked. He had closed his bag, but he did not look up.

'Yes,' Philip said. 'Saturday's a big day. My dad's bringing Alex and Viki in our car. It's really strange. He has enough money to help support the basketball team–'

'Philip! You asked him to do that. You wanted him to promise* money every month like some of the other parents,' Viki said.

'As I was saying, it's really strange. My dad has money for the team, but he doesn't have enough money to get the software I need. I'm going to start writing my own computer games,' Philip said to Chris and Steve.

'Philip!' Viki could not believe her brother was talking about their father like this. These people were not even family.

'It's true, Vik,' said Philip. 'He spends money on things that are not important. He can't see that we must learn how to use computers in lots of different ways. We'll never get jobs if we don't.'

'Did you tell him that?' asked Chris.

'Of course I did. *And* I told him he lives in the past,' said Philip.

The other boys looked at him, their eyes wide open. 'Weren't you ... afraid?' Steve asked.

'I'm not afraid of my dad,' said Philip. He seemed to get taller.

Viki could not listen to this any more. 'Don't talk like that,' she shouted. 'Maybe you're not afraid of Dad, but you should care about him. He does everything he can for you. And all *you* can do is say bad things about him to your friends!' Viki's face was as white as her shirt.

'Hey, Viki.' said Steve. 'We all know your dad's a great guy.'

'Relax, relax,' Barbara said quietly. 'Phil's only giving an opinion.'

'Viki, I know Dad tries hard. But life is changing so fast,' Philip said calmly. 'They decided what we should learn in school fifteen years ago. There wasn't much need for computers then. But it's all changed now. In a year or two you'll leave school. If you want to work, you'll need to know about them, too.'

'You just want to go on playing more and more games. I see you at home, Philip, playing for hours and hours. You can't live without those stupid games. Of course, you can't lose with a computer game, can you? You can only win and go on getting better and winning more. That's not work! That's not making money! That's just boys with toys*!' Viki walked out into the rain, away from her brother and his friends.

'You'll catch cold,' Chris said.

Steve followed Viki. He took her arm and brought her back under the tree.

Philip was talking to Chris.

'She's right about some of it,' Philip said. 'I do enjoy the games. But I want to use the computer for work, too. And I do want to be a programmer when I leave school.'

'Then explain to Dad. Don't just get angry!' Viki said, more quietly.

'Oh Viki!' Chris said. 'You tell Philip not to get angry, but what did you do just now?'

Barbara smiled. 'It must be a family thing. Even your mouth went white.'

Viki walked out into the rain, away from her brother and friends.

Viki relaxed and smiled a little, too. 'Oh no. Philip and Dad go red when they're angry,' she said. The others laughed.

'My bus!' Barbara said suddenly. She kissed Viki and Philip quickly and ran to the bus stop with lots of other students.

'Bye,' she called.

'Come on,' Chris said. 'Let's go, too. A little rain won't hurt us.'

They walked along the road, Viki between Philip and Chris, Steve walking behind.

'Have you got your umbrella*, Steve?' Philip asked, turning his head. 'Viki's getting wet.'

'No, not today,' Steve felt stupid and sad. 'Sorry.' He tried to walk beside them, but the road was not wide enough.

'It's OK,' Viki said without turning round. 'My coat's already wet.'

CHAPTER **3**

Thursday evening: training

'Jump, Red Six, jump!' Luke, the new trainer, shouted across the basketball court.

Philip, wearing number six on his red shirt, jumped again and hit the ball out of another boy's hands. It flew straight at Chris. Chris held it, turned and started running to the other end of the court.

'Pass it,' Luke called. 'Give it to Red Six.'

Philip's father, Jim, walked along the side of the court to where Luke was jumping up and down and shouting to the players. Luke was a short man, but he had a loud voice and a big smile.

When he saw Jim, he said 'Hi,' and turned back to the training match.

'Shoot, Red Fourteen, shoot! ... No, no. Don't forget the guards. Stop, stop. Relax a minute, boys. Take five*.' He turned back to Jim. 'Thanks for coming,' he said. 'It's good that there are ten boys. We've made two teams and I can really see what's good and what's bad. Are you sure you can come on Saturday?'

'Oh yes, no problem,' answered Jim. 'But you said something about money on the phone.'

'Yeah.' Luke smiled. 'We're going to need more money this time to pay for the minibus and things. And the other team wants us to pay half for the referee* and the court caretaker*.'

Jim was surprised. 'We've never paid a caretaker before,' he said. 'Are you sure?'

'That's what they told me,' Luke said. 'Look, I don't know why, but there's almost no money in the bank for your team. I can't organise away matches without money.'

'No, of course not,' Jim said. 'But there was quite a lot in the bank last time I used the bank book.'

'When was that?' Luke asked, looking at the boys. They were sitting at the side of the court, drinking

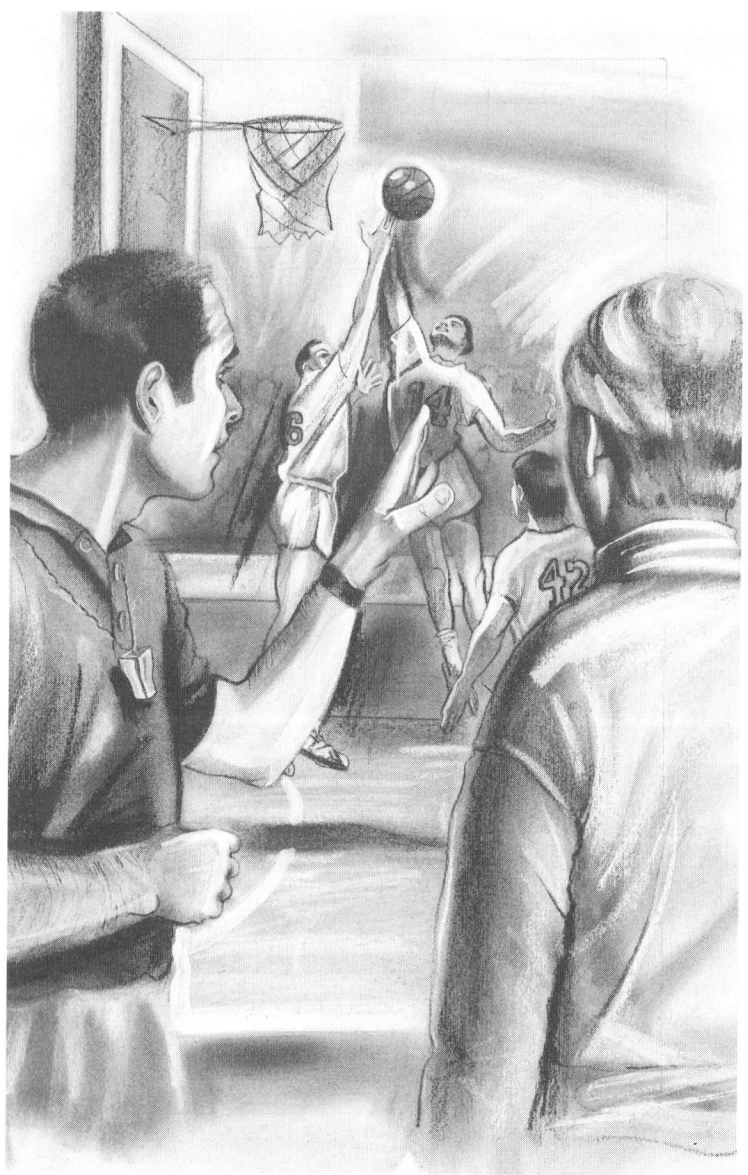

Luke and Jim watched from the side of the court. 'Shoot, Red Fourteen, shoot!' Luke called.

water from plastic bottles and laughing. Viki, Barbara and another girl were sitting with them. They had come to watch the boys' training session.

'OK,' Luke shouted. 'Back on the court.' They started to get up.

'Maybe a month ago,' Jim answered.

'Before the other trainer left,' Luke said. He looked at Jim with a little smile.

'True,' Jim said. 'Do you think he...?'

'Look, Jim, I don't think anything. I just have a job to do – and I need help from you and the other parents to do it well. OK?'

'Yes, of course, of course. I know you're busy. Work the boys hard!' and he smiled at Luke as he walked away.

Jim stood near the corner of the court, watching. He decided that he must talk to some of the other fathers in the next few days.

Viki came and stood beside him.

'What's Luke like?' she asked. 'He looks really nice and the boys think he's great.'

'He seems very good,' her father said. 'We'll see how it goes on Saturday. We need to win. If we don't, we'll go down to the second division at the end of the year. Let's hope he's the best!'

⑤

CHAPTER **4**

Thursday evening: work

Later that evening, Penny was putting on her coat near the front door.

'Alex is sleeping, Viki has gone to bed and Philip is playing on the computer,' she said to Jim. 'I should be back about midnight.'

'You don't have to do this,' Jim said to her. 'I don't like it. And I don't like telling the children you're at my mother's when you're cleaning shops.'

'Well, my love, it won't be forever,' Penny said with a big smile. 'Next year, when Alex is at school all day, I'll stop.' She gave him a big kiss and went out.

Penny walked to the shop.

'He's right, of course,' she thought. 'We're not rich, but we have enough for the house and clothes and good food. We don't have much extra, it's true. What I make only pays for the car. Ah well ... Now Alex is at school in the mornings, so maybe I can get a morning job in a pharmacy again. Somehow I just can't tell the children I work as a cleaner. Viki says that cleaning is the worst thing you can do. She doesn't understand that we need the money and there is no other work at night.'

The shop she cleaned on Thursdays and Saturdays belonged to Mr Levendis. She used her key to get in and he was in the back room.

'Hello!' she called.

'Good evening, Mrs Alexiou. How are you?' Mr Levendis answered.

'Fine, thanks. I'll start in the top room, shall I?'

Mr Levendis came out into the main shop.

'Yes, that's fine,' he said. 'I'll finish down here and leave in a few minutes.' Penny wanted to talk to him about an idea she had had. But he seemed to be in a hurry*. He said, 'I have to get home early tonight. We are having a family party for my son's birthday.'

'Oh, how nice!' said Penny. 'Wish him a happy ... oh no, of course. Don't say anything. He doesn't know I'm here.'

'You can wish him a happy birthday yourself when you take Alex to school tomorrow morning.' Mr Levendis smiled at her. He was a thin man with a tired face. He said he wore glasses because he spent all day looking at computers in his shop. But he had had them since he was seven years old. Now he took them off and cleaned them.

'You don't need to feel bad about working here, Mrs Alexiou. I keep your secret because you want me to. But no one will think badly of you if you tell people.'

'You are very kind. Let's keep the secret a little longer ... But I did want to ask you–'

'OK, then. Look, I must be quick. I'll see you again on Saturday.'

'Of course. And thank you, Mr Levendis,' Penny said. He walked into the back room again. 'I'll have to talk to him on Saturday,' she thought.

She began working, singing quietly to herself as she cleaned. She heard the door open and looked down to see who it was. It was a man she had never seen before.

'Harris, you here?' the man called. His hair was dark, but on top it was getting a bit thin. Mr Levendis came out.

'Yes. I was just leaving. Are you coming to little John's party?'

'I wanted to make one or two phone calls, if that's OK. I'll come on after that,' the man said.

'Of course.' The man went into the back office. Mr Levendis looked up at Penny for a second. He called to the man, 'Lock the door when you leave and bring me the keys.'

'OK,' said the man and Mr Levendis left.

Penny stayed still. She could hear the man speaking quietly on the telephone. After a few moments he began to speak more loudly.

'I can get another ten, but no more,' he was saying. 'You said that was enough yesterday. Why are you changing it now?'

There was silence for a moment. 'A hundred thousand drachmas! No one gets a hundred thousand. We agreed fifty and now you want double.' Another silence. 'Don't play with me. Be careful, or maybe things will not go so well for you. I'll meet you at George's after the match and give you the money … OK. Bye.'

Mr Levendis looked up at Penny for a second.

Penny heard the man talking quietly to himself. He tried another telephone number. It seemed there was no answer. He turned off the lights and left. Penny waited five minutes. Then she put the lights back on and started work again.

When she had finished, she remembered her idea. She wrote Mr Levendis a note. The note said that she wanted to talk about something with him on Saturday afternoon. Then she went home. It was eleven forty-five.

CHAPTER **5**

Saturday: on the road

'Mum! Where's my red shirt?' Philip shouted. 'I need my red shirt.'

Penny came into Philip's room. 'It's in your bag with the other things for the match. Relax, Philip. Everything is there.'

Philip took everything out of his bag, found the shirt and put everything back again. 'OK,' he said without looking up.

Penny walked out of his room without speaking. She was getting tired of Philip's problems. He had changed, and she didn't know what to say to him any more. Jim had only spoken to him once or twice since Sunday.

In the kitchen she found Jim. He was making sandwiches for the journey. Alex came running in and said, 'It's raining, Dad. Are we going?'

'A little rain doesn't usually stop a match,' Jim said.

The phone rang*. It was Luke. He said, 'There's a storm coming up, but it's moving fast. We'll leave as soon as we can.'

'OK,' Jim said. He put the phone down. 'Come on, everyone. We're leaving.'

'I'll sit by Dad in the front,' Viki said to Philip, as they were getting into the car.

'Today, Viki my love, I prefer to have Philip next to me,' Jim said kindly. 'I know you won't talk to me, Philip. But maybe I will talk to you.'

So Viki got into the car behind her father with Alex beside her. Philip seemed angry. He sat silently beside his father.

'We're meeting the minibus and the rest of the team at our basketball court in five minutes,' Jim said.

'Goodbye, Mum,' Alex shouted, looking out of the back window.

'Good luck,' Penny called. 'And drive carefully!'

They followed the minibus along the road out of town with the sea on their left and the mountains on their right. The rain was not heavy, but the wind was very strong. They could see more mountains across the sea. Sometimes the sun came out between the dark clouds. It made the sea very bright for a moment or two.

The road went through two villages and then started going up. On the left, the land was rocky straight down to the sea. On the right, the mountain was like a wall.

'Hey, look!' Alex said, his eyes on the sea.

They saw a flash of lightning hit the sea. A few seconds later they heard the roll of thunder in the distance.

'The storm's a long way away,' Jim said.

'How far is it to the match, Dad?' Alex asked.

'About an hour's drive,' Jim answered.

They went round a bend* to the right. A small river ran down the mountain. The rain had made it bigger and it ran over the road. They drove through it fast and the water went everywhere.

'Whee!' shouted Alex, and even Philip laughed.

Viki saw a sign by the road.

'Look, Dad,' she said. 'It says it rains rocks here!'

'Not today I hope,' said Jim with a laugh. 'We have important business!'

They drove round another bend. The minibus had stopped in the middle of the road. Jim had to stop very suddenly. It was dangerous on the wet road. The minibus driver was pushing a big rock to the side. It had fallen from the mountain to their right.

Philip opened his window and shouted, 'What's the matter?'

'Just a rock come down with the rain,' the driver called back. 'It's OK now.' He turned back to the minibus. A sudden flash of lightning made everything white and a crash of thunder hurt their ears.

They saw a flash of lightning hit the sea.

The driver started to run, but another noise made him look up at the mountain. Suddenly, hundreds of rocks, large and small, were flying through the air. They were coming down on the road. They pushed the minibus over onto its side. There was a terrible noise of people screaming* and glass breaking. Rocks rained through the open car window onto Philip. One smashed* the window beside Alex. The car was pushed to the side of the road above the sea. Some rocks flew right over the road and fell into the water.

Then the terrible noise stopped. And the only sound was the falling rain.

CHAPTER **6**

Saturday: during the storm

Jim turned and looked at his children. Philip was badly hurt. There was blood on his face and his arm looked broken. He was covered in rocks and dirt. His eyes were shut and he was not moving.

When Jim turned round to Viki she looked back at him. Her eyes and her mouth were wide open. 'Are you alright?' he asked. She moved her head to say yes.

Jim looked at Alex. He could only see the boy's back. Alex had turned away from the window and pushed his face into the seat*. There were rocks and glass and dirt all over him.

'Alex?' Jim said. 'Are you OK?'

Alex moved a little. 'Yes, I think so,' he said. 'Has it stopped?'

'Yes, it has.'

'What happened?'

'It was a landslide*,' Jim said. 'Viki, Philip is badly hurt and we must get help very soon.' Jim's voice was very quiet. His face was white. He moved some of the dirt and rocks from Philip's jacket. He put his head down and listened for Philip's heart.

Viki said in a very small voice, 'Is Phil...?'

'No, he's not dead. I can hear his heart,' Jim said. 'I'm going to get out and see what's happening. I want you to help Alex get out and see if he's hurt. Then stay with Phil. I'll be back soon.'

'OK,' Viki said. She opened her door slowly. The car was very near to the side of the road. She could see the sea crashing on the rocks below.

'Come on, Alex,' she said. 'You'll have to be careful. We might fall into the sea from here.'

Alex moved along the seat. Dirt and glass fell off his back. He got out and looked out at the sea. 'Ooh ... we're lucky the car didn't go over.' He and Viki got round to the other side of the car.

'We must try to get some of these rocks away from the doors,' she said. 'We can't help Phil until we can open his door.' The two children started moving rocks in the rain.

Jim ran over the top of the fallen rocks to the driver.

Viki could see the sea crashing on the rocks below.

He could only see some hair. He carefully began to move the rocks. The driver suddenly made a noise. Now Jim could see him. The rain was washing away the dirt from his face.

'Are you all right?' Jim asked.

'I think so, but I can't move. I don't know if anything is broken,' he said.

'I'll try and get someone from the bus. I need help to move all these,' Jim said.

'Luke,' he shouted.

'Yes, Jim. I'm here,' Luke shouted back from inside the bus.

'Are you hurt? Can you push the door open?'

'I'm trying ... Come on, boys. We've got to get out of here. Push!' And, with Jim's help, the door moved at last.

Luke was the first to get out. He jumped away from the minibus and started using his mobile phone. Jim helped Steve and Chris out. They seemed to be OK. No one seemed to be seriously hurt, but most of the boys had cuts and contusions*. Jim told Steve to shut the door to stop the rain getting into the bus. Then Steve went straight to the driver and began moving the rocks and dirt off him.

Jim shouted to Luke, 'Have you phoned the ambulance?'

'What? No, no,' Luke answered. 'I'm trying to talk to ... er ... I have to tell someone that the match is not going to happen. Hello, hello? Ben, are you there? ... Nothing. Stupid machine!'

Jim could not believe that Luke was not calling either

an ambulance or the police. 'Give me that phone,' he shouted at Luke.

'I have to talk to Ben,' Luke said. 'Then you can have the phone.'

'Are you crazy?!' Jim shouted. He tried to take the phone from Luke, but couldn't. Jim pushed Luke and the phone fell from Luke's hand. Jim immediately picked it up and called the emergency services. Nothing happened.

Chris took out his mobile phone. He turned it on, but nothing came up on the display.

'The battery is dead,' he said. He was almost crying. 'Oh, how stupid.' He went back to the bus.

Jim tried again with Luke's phone. Then he gave it back to Luke. 'It isn't working,' he said. 'Maybe the rain has got into it. Try and make it work – and call the emergency services!'

The driver was now sitting up.

'I think he has broken his left leg,' Steve said to Jim. 'Come and see.'

'How do you feel?' Jim asked the driver.

'Not so bad. My left leg feels dead, but nothing else seems wrong.' He tried to get up.

Jim could see the leg was probably broken.

'Hey, you stay here a minute,' he said. 'I'll get you into the car as soon as I can. I'll send someone for an ambulance.'

He looked over at Viki and Alex. They had moved a lot of rocks away from the car. Steve was helping them now. Chris was standing in the rain watching them and

Jim pushed Luke and the phone fell from Luke's hand.

Luke was trying to get back into the bus.

'Someone must go back to the nearest village for help,' Jim shouted. 'Philip is badly hurt and the driver has a broken leg.'

Luke got down into the bus. Chris was looking at the sea. The noise of the rain was very loud.

'I'll go,' Steve said to Jim.

'Thank you, Steve. We need someone to go with you. It's safer if two people go.' He looked at the bus again. 'Everyone in the bus is hurt. Most of them are not too bad, but only Luke and Chris are completely OK.' He called to the others, 'Who can go with Steve for help?'

Chris walked to the side of the road and suddenly vomited. His face was green. Luke had disappeared through the door of the bus.

'I'll go with Steve,' Viki said to her father. 'We'll run. It was only three or four kilometres back. We may meet a car coming this way. Alex needs help with Philip, Dad. He hasn't moved.'

'OK. You go carefully and I'll take care of* Philip and the driver.'

Steve touched Viki's arm. 'Come on,' he said. 'Fast but careful, like on a motorbike...'

She smiled at him and they started running down the empty road. Far away, over the sea, the sun came through the clouds for a moment.

Far away, over the sea, the sun came through the clouds for a moment.

CHAPTER **7**

Saturday: waiting for help

Jim closed Philip's window and covered his son with a jacket. He asked Alex to clean out the back of the car now that they could open the door. He told Luke to get the bus driver ready to move. He told Chris to get back in the bus and find something to cover the broken windows. Then Luke and Jim carried the bus driver to the car.

Jim helped the bus driver into the back seat. 'Are you comfortable?' he asked.

'Better than sitting on a bed of rocks in the rain,' the driver said. 'But I have never been so wet.'

Alex sat in the driver's seat beside Philip. He dried his brother's hair a little and put another jacket over him.

At that moment Philip woke up. He opened his eyes and looked at Alex beside him.

'Hello, Alex,' he said.

Alex laughed. 'You're OK,' he said.

Jim went round to Philip's door and opened it. He took Philip's good hand in his. He tried to say something, but he could not speak.

Philip smiled a little.

'My arm hurts a l-l-lot and I'm really c-c-cold. What happened, Dad? Was Alex driving and we hit the m-m-mountain?'

Jim started to cry. He held Philip's hand and put his head down and cried like a baby.

'Hey, Dad,' Alex said. 'Are you crying because Philip's OK? I know you don't like each other much, but I didn't know it was so bad! Don't be sad, Phil. Mum will be happy that you're OK, even if Dad isn't.'

Jim's face was wet when he looked up, but he was laughing. 'You be careful, young man,' he said to Alex. 'Your bottom will hurt you when I catch you later.'

'Oh, it hurts enough now,' Alex said seriously. 'It has pieces of glass in it, I think.'

Philip started to laugh. 'Ow!' he said. 'My arm really d-d-does hurt. Don't make me laugh.'

'I know how to stop you laughing,' Alex said. 'Just think about how long you will have to wait until you can play a computer game again!'

'Or basketball,' their father said, sadly. 'Look, I must start the car and get Philip and the driver warmer. Viki and Steve have gone for help.' He shut Philip's door and covered the broken back window with someone's jacket. The car started first time and they all began to feel warmer.

■ ■ ■

Steve and Viki came to the little river and slowed down. There was a lot of water running across the road. They stopped for a few moments' rest. When they could speak, Steve said, 'You like Chris a lot, don't you?'

Viki walked straight into the water. It came almost to her knees. She turned to him and said, 'Come on. Remember Philip.' Steve ran through the water and they went on down the road.

They came round a bend. Below them they saw a restaurant under some big trees. Further away, a lot of water was running across the road. It made a deep river. People were sitting in their cars on the other side. They were waiting for the rain to stop and the water to go down.

'That restaurant must have a phone,' Viki shouted. She began to run faster down the last piece of road. Suddenly, she cried out and fell down. Steve came up to her fast. She was sitting on the road, holding her foot.

'Oh, how stupid!' she said, looking up at Steve. 'I've hurt my foot. Run, Steve, run and phone the hospital. We don't know if Philip will live. Go on, go on!'

'I'm going,' Steve said. 'But do you need help?'

'No, no, I'm OK. Just go, Steve, go, go...' Viki was crying. She could not talk. She began pushing herself on her bottom to the side of the road.

CHAPTER **8**

Saturday: help arrives

Steve turned and ran the short distance to the restaurant. He ran in and stopped. He could not see anyone.

'Is something wrong, young man?' A quiet, old voice came from the dark back room.

'There's been a bad accident up on the coast road. There was a landslide. I–I need to call an–an ambulance, and maybe the police.' In the darkness, Steve saw an old woman. She was sitting at a table, preparing food.

'I'll call my son,' she said. 'You sit down for a minute.' She shouted, 'George! Come here now, immediately. There's been an accident.'

George came in. He was a very big man with grey hair and a moustache. He looked at Steve and saw a thin boy, all wet, his face very white. George brought the telephone and a chair and sat beside him. 'OK, young man,' he said. 'Tell me what you need.'

George called the ambulance and then the police. It was all done in five minutes. Steve went out to Viki.

She was sitting on the wet ground under a tree. The rain had stopped. Steve sat down beside her. He looked at his feet.

'The ambulance is coming,' he said. 'The man from the restaurant will drive us back to the others in a few minutes.'

'Oh, Steve, thank you.' She wanted to cry again but stopped herself. Steve looked up at her.

'You don't need to thank me.' They were silent.

Then he said, 'How's your foot?'

'It hurts,' she said.

George came out with his two sons. He picked Viki up and put her in the front of his truck. Then the two sons and Steve got in the back and George drove up the road to the accident.

'George!' she shouted. 'Come here now, immediately. There's been an accident.'

■ ■ ■

Philip and the bus driver were as comfortable as possible as they waited for help. Jim went to see what was happening in the overturned bus. The rain had stopped and the door was open. He looked in. Everyone was sitting down.

Someone had turned on the radio and most of the boys were singing with it. The song finished and the presenter said, 'We have some sports news. A junior men's basketball match was planned for this afternoon at the Louis Sports Centre. Well, it's not going to happen. Not today, anyway. The police tell us that the visiting team has been stopped by a landslide during the storm. We hope no one has been hurt.

'When the team does get here,' he went on, 'we'll be ready for them. Our team can't lose.'

The boys in the bus started shouting, 'You'll see who can't lose' and 'Don't be so sure'. Even the two boys who had the worst cuts were laughing. Luke was looking at the floor. There was a strange smile on his face. But when he saw Jim watching him, he began laughing with the boys.

'The police know,' Jim said to himself, 'so Steve and Viki have contacted them. They'll be here soon.'

■ ■ ■

He heard a truck coming round the bend. He ran back to his car. As George jumped down from the truck, they heard the ambulance siren as it started up the mountain road.

43

Everyone was sitting down and singing in the overturned bus.

CHAPTER 9

Saturday night

'You can see your son now,' said the doctor. 'His arm will be fine in a few weeks and he can leave hospital tomorrow.'

'Thank you, Doctor,' Jim said. 'That's marvellous news.' He pushed open the door and went in.

Philip was sitting up in bed. His face was white and his eyes were dark. They seemed larger than usual. He looked up at Jim, but he did not speak.

'The doctor says you'll be ready to come home tomorrow,' Jim said.

'It'll be better than here,' Philip said. 'But what am I going to do?'

Jim moved a chair close to Philip's bed and sat down.

'Now this has happened,' he said, 'I really wish I could buy you what you want. I sometimes–'

'Dad, Dad, I didn't mean...' Philip started to speak.

'No, Phil, listen. I sometimes find it very difficult to know what is best. And I can't buy everything we all want. I want to, but I can't. In fact, your mother–'

At that moment Penny came in. She ran over to Philip and kissed him. Then she looked at him carefully.

'You're OK,' she said.

'Hi, Mum. Yes, I've got a broken arm and I have to stay in bed for a week. I can't play computer games or basketball for weeks, perhaps months. But I'm OK.'

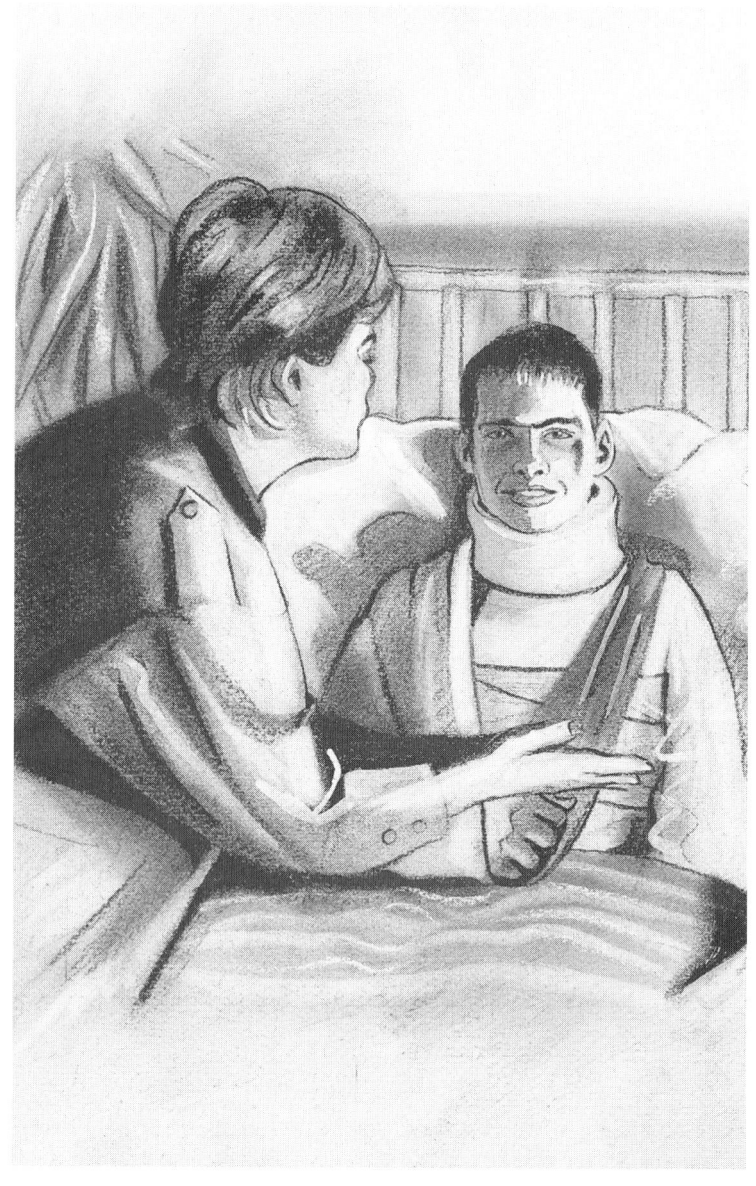

Penny ran over to Philip and kissed him.

Penny laughed. 'Oh yes. You're fine. A week in bed will give you the chance to study for those exams in June.' She turned to Jim. 'How are the others? Where are they?'

'Viki has hurt her foot and will have to rest it for a month,' Jim said. 'Alex has bad contusions on his back and his bottom, but no other problems. They're with Steve and Barbara in the waiting room. The doctor said they can go home now. But Philip must spend the night here. He's taking some special medicine.'

'What a story!' Penny said. 'I'll stay with Phil until he sleeps. Bring the others in. They can see him for a minute and then you can take them home. You need a good wash!'

■ ■ ■

When everyone else had gone, Penny spoke to Philip.

'Phil, do you really feel OK?'

'Not too bad, Mum. They gave me all kinds of medicine.'

'Because if you're well enough,' Penny said, 'there's something I want to ask you. What do you know about your trainer, Luke Makris?'

'Not much. He's doing a good job with the team. He rides a big motorbike. That's about all. Why?' Philip asked.

'I saw him just now at the hospital reception. And I had seen him once before,' his mother answered. 'I saw him before when he was making a phone call and I heard what he said. He was having a disagreement with someone. I think I understand what it was about now. Someone wanted a lot of money. They had agreed on fifty thousand and then the other man wanted a hundred. Luke said it was impossible.'

'What are you talking about?' Philip was completely confused.

'Was Luke paying the referee to make sure your team won the match? Is that why Luke said on the phone, "Make sure they win"? Do you think that's possible, Philip?'

'I ... I don't know. It's possible, yes, maybe,' Philip said. 'I have heard of that kind of thing. But not in our kind of basketball. And why? No one makes any money from our matches.'

'That's what I wanted to ask you. Why? We need to know more about Mr Luke Makris, I think,' Penny said. 'And I know someone who knows him. I'm going to make a phone call. I won't be long.'

CHAPTER 10
...and Sunday morning

Jim went to the hospital on Sunday morning to bring Philip back home.

In the car Jim said, 'The doctor says you mustn't write with your right hand for at least a month, maybe six weeks. But you should be OK in time for the exams.'

Philip was looking at the road in front. 'I thought about that last night. I didn't sleep much. At first I was happy I had broken my arm. I thought I could miss* the exams. But later I understood that Mum was right. Before she left, she said I am lucky to be alive. She said you and Viki and Steve probably saved my life. She's right ... Thanks.'

Jim was surprised and happy. He said, 'I had to make sure you were OK. Maybe you don't believe it, but you are important to me.'

They drove on in silence.

As he came into the kitchen and saw his mother, Philip laughed.

'It's good to be home,' he said. Penny smiled at him and winked*.

'Come and sit down,' Penny said to Jim and Philip. 'Children!' she shouted. 'Come and tell me all about what happened yesterday.'

Viki and Alex came in and sat down.

'I want to hear the whole story again,' Penny said.

Alex described the journey and the landslide. Viki told everyone how she and Steve ran for help and found George and his sons.

'I had to sit in the truck and watch,' Viki said. 'I couldn't help because of my foot. George and his two sons helped to move the rocks round our car. Philip stayed in the car, but they put the bus driver in the ambulance. We followed the ambulance. Oh, and two boys from the bus went in the ambulance as well. At the hospital the doctors took care of everyone.'

'It seems,' Jim said, 'that we were unlucky. No cars came from our direction because the road was under water near George's restaurant. And no cars came the other way because there was another landslide in front of us. The police said the other landslide wasn't as bad as ours, but it obstructed the road. It was the worst storm for twenty years.'

'Now I want to ask another question,' Penny said. At that moment the door bell* rang. 'Ah, that must be Mr Levendis.'

Philip laughed.

'What's happening, Phil?' his father asked.

'I'm not sure, Dad. But I think Mr Levendis is going to tell us.'

Barbara was with Mr Levendis. She came in and sat beside Philip. He took her hand and held it.

'Jim,' Penny said. 'This is Mr Harris Levendis. I clean his computer shop on Thursdays and Saturdays.'

'What!' Viki and Alex shouted together. 'What do you mean?' Viki said. 'You're a pharmacist, not a cleaner!'

'I've been a cleaner for two or three years now. I was – well, I felt bad about it, so I didn't tell you. But soon I shall have another kind of job. As I said, Mr Levendis has a computer shop. He also has a cousin called Luke Makris.'

'Our trainer?' Jim said.

'That's right, Mr Alexiou,' said Mr Levendis. 'He is my cousin. But he's done some very stupid things. I

'What!' Viki and Alex shouted together. 'You're a pharmacist, not a cleaner!'

need to talk to you and the other parents about them. He took money from you all to pay the referee of yesterday's match. He wanted to be the trainer for the national Under 18s team. So he "organised" all his matches. His teams never lost. But now he is going to tell the Athletics Foundation about what he has done. I thought it was strange that his teams always won. But he *is* my cousin ... and I wasn't sure. Mrs Alexiou was in the shop last Thursday. She heard him making an agreement with a referee on the telephone. So now we can be sure. It's very sad. He'll never be a trainer again. Maybe he'll even go to prison.'

Everyone was quiet for a moment.

'At the landslide, in the rain,' Jim said, 'he didn't want to call the emergency services. He was phoning someone called Ben. The referee's name is Ben Pappas. Now I understand what he was doing.'

Philip said, 'He told us at training, "With me you can't lose." I thought he meant we are good because we try so hard. But he was buying our matches. We are good enough to win without that. Why didn't he believe it?'

'Perhaps the team will cost you less now Dad,' Viki said.

Penny laughed. 'Then you can have your new disco dress, eh, Viki?'

'Mm...hm,' Viki said with a smile.

'And Phil can have his software,' Alex said. 'And I can play his games.'

'Don't go so fast,' Jim said. He was laughing.

'Well,' Mr Levendis said. 'I have an idea about that. Mrs Alexiou showed me an article about a computer café in New York. I think she found it in your room, Philip.' Mr Levendis took off his glasses and cleaned them.

'I didn't know you read my computer magazines, Mum,' Philip said.

'I don't understand most of it. And I don't look for things in your room. But this was on your bed one day. So I read it.'

The telephone rang. Viki answered it. It was Steve. She smiled and took the telephone into her room.

Mr Levendis went on. 'Not many people know about computers in our town. I think the computer café is a very good idea. People can come and have coffee and cakes, and look at the computer magazines. I will teach them how to use computers and what they can do. Then I will sell more computers and more software. There is just one problem...' Mr Levendis looked at Penny. She smiled.

'I shall need two people to work for me – one in the café and one to help me teach people about computers. Do you know anyone who could do that, Philip?'

'I ... er ... I ... well, I could, I think,' Philip said. Everyone laughed.

'I've seen what you do on your own computer and I phoned your head teacher this morning. He thinks you will pass your school exams in June. If you do well and

People can come and have coffee and cakes, and look at the computer magazines.

your father agrees, then I think you are the right person.'

'I agree,' Jim said quickly. Philip laughed. 'Thanks, Dad,' he said.

'And I would like Mrs Alexiou to think about taking care of the café for me. It's not a pharmacy, but I hope it will be a good place to work.'

'Oh, Mr Levendis. You know I'd like to,' Penny said. 'I really must say a big "thank you" to you for everything. Come and have lunch with us now. You, too, Barbara. We always have a family lunch on Sundays. Just salad, meat and chips with fruit salad and ice-cream to follow. It's always the same, isn't it, Philip?'

Philip smiled. 'That's right. The food never changes. But this Sunday I have to eat with my left hand and Alex can't sit down. It is a *little* different from last Sunday.'

CHAPTER 11   12

Epilogue

In June, Harris Levendis came to Sunday lunch again.

'Well, Philip,' he said. 'Now your arm is OK and the exams are over, I want you to come to the shop next weekend. You need to learn all the machines and software. We open the following Monday. I'm on the internet now so you will need to know all about that, too. I'll teach you how on Sunday.'

'It sounds more like a new world than a new job, Phil,' Jim said.

'When I know everything, I'll teach you, Dad,' said Philip.

'Harris, I must thank you for giving Philip this chance,' Jim said. 'It has changed his life.'

'You must thank your wife, not me,' said Mr Levendis. 'But I have to thank you for helping me with my cousin. The basketball association have stopped him from being a trainer. The police want to talk to him. If he tells the truth, I don't think he will go to prison. But all of his teams will have to play their matches again. Maybe he will have to pay for that. Has the new trainer started?'

'Yes, I've seen him,' Alex said. 'He shouts a lot, too, but he's been to America and he drives an old Mustang. He's OK.'

E X E R C I S E S

A Comprehension

Chapter 1 Answer yes or no to these questions.

1 Is the family rich?
2 Is Jim angry with Philip?
3 Is Viki's basketball match on Wednesday?
4 Is Philip angry because he can't have the new computer program he wants?
5 Is Philip's basketball match in their town?
6 Does Philip know what kind of job he wants to get when he leaves school?

Chapter 2 Answer these questions with a name.

1 Which boy does Viki like?
2 Who was given a mobile phone?
3 Which boy likes Viki a lot?
4 Who will bring some friends to the Wednesday match?
5 Who gives money to Philip's basketball team?

Chapters 3 and 4

1 Who asked Jim to come to the training session?
2 What does Luke need from Jim?
3 Where does the team keep its money?
4 Why is Saturday's match important?
5 What work does Penny do?
6 Do her children know that she works?
7 Why is Mr Levendis in a hurry?
8 What does the man in the shop talk about on the phone?

Chapters 5 and 6

1 Why does Viki say she will sit in the front beside Jim?
2 What makes Philip laugh during the drive?
3 Who opened the window and called to the minibus driver?
4 What made the rocks begin falling?
5 Who was badly hurt by the rocks?
6 Who was not hurt?

7 Did Luke call an ambulance?
8 Why didn't Chris's mobile phone work?
9 How did Chris feel?
10 Who ran for help?

Chapters 7 and 8

1 Who took control of the situation?
2 Why do you think Jim began crying?
3 How did Jim get the people in the car warmer?
4 What happened when Viki ran down the hill to the restaurant?
5 How did Steve and Viki get back to the landslide?
6 How did Jim learn that Steve and Viki had contacted the police?
7 What was Luke's expression when the boys in the bus were shouting at the radio?
8 What could they hear coming up the mountain as George's truck arrived?

Chapters 9-11

1 Who was the man Penny heard talking on the phone?
2 What does Penny think he was talking about?
3 Who does she telephone from the hospital that evening?
4 What did Philip understand during his night without sleep?
5 Who is Mr Levendis's cousin?
6 What will happen to Luke Makris?
7 What changes is Mr Levendis going to make to his shop?
8 Who is going to help him?

B Working with Language

1 **Use these prepositions to complete the sentences below.**

in   into   on   onto   at

1 You moved … that big house last year.
2 We're meeting the minibus … five minutes.
3 They pushed the minibus over … its side.
4 Shut the door to stop the rain getting … the bus.

5 Are you coming … Saturday?

6 I'll change my job next year, when Alex is … school all day.

7 I heard him talking to someone … the phone.

8 I have to stay … bed for a week.

9 … the hospital, the doctors took care of everyone.

10 Jim helped the driver … the back seat of the car

2 Use the words given in brackets to join the pairs of sentences below.

before   while   until   when   after

1 …George had made the phone calls, Steve went out to wait with Viki.

2 …Luke was making his phone calls, Penny stayed still.

3 …Philip came back to the empty kitchen, Alex had eaten all the ice-cream.

4 Philip stayed in bed … he was better

5 The rain stopped … George and his sons arrived to help.

6 …the driver sat up, they found he had broken his left leg.

7 Penny didn't know that Mr Levendis's cousin was Luke Makris … she saw him at the hospital.

8 Penny went to work … the children had gone to bed.

9 Philip always played games on his computer … Sunday lunch.

10 …they were waiting for help to arrive, the boys in the bus sang songs.

C Activities

1 When do you think this story took place? Find the quotations from the story to support your date.

2 Write a short paragraph about how technology has changed since the time of the story.

3 Have any natural disasters happened in the area where you live? Find out about a local disaster. Write a short newspaper report about it. Find a photograph or draw a picture to illustrate your report.

4 It is the week after the storm. Alex has to write an essay about the landslide for his class teacher. Write his essay for him.

5 You are either a player or a spectator at a sports match. Write a report of the match. Say if you enjoyed the match or not.

6 Describe how Philip's character develops during the story.

GLOSSARY

at home *(adv)* you play at home when you play on your own ground, at your own school or stadium

away *(adv)* you play away when you go to the other team[*]'s ground

bang *(n)* a loud noise

bell *(n)* when someone comes to your door, they ring[*] the door *bell* to get your attention

bend *(n)* a curve in the road

caretaker *(n)* a *caretaker* takes care of[*] a building or other place, here, a basketball court

contusion *(n)* an injury that changes skin colour, usually red or blue

guy *(n)* informal word for man or boy

in a hurry *(exp)* not have much time

keep out of *(v)* here, take refuge from (the rain)

landslide *(n)* where a section of land breaks away from the side of a hill or mountain and moves downwards

match *(n)* a game between two teams[*]

minibus *(n)* a small bus

miss *(v)* here, to not do (the exams)

parents *(pl n)* mother and father

promise *(v)* say you will do something

referee *(n)* the person who arbitrates during a match

ring *(v)* the telephone *rings* when someone is calling you; past tense *rang*

roll of thunder *(n)* a deep sound in the sky during a storm; *thunder* follows lightning

score *(n)* the number of points you or your team[*] win in a game

scream *(v)* to cry out in pain or because you are afraid

seat *(n)* a place to sit; here, a car *seat*

shout *(v)* to speak very loudly, often in anger or fear

smash *(v)* to break into small pieces with a loud noise

support *(v)* to provide moral, financial or other help

take care of *(v)* to be responsible for

take five *(exp)* have five minutes to relax

team *(n)* a group of players who play together

toy *(n)* a thing to play with

trainer *(n)* a person who teaches athletes

training *(n)* in sport, learning better technique and working regularly to make your body stronger

umbrella *(n)* you hold an *umbrella* over your head to keep dry in the rain

wink *(v)* to quickly close and open one eye

Richmond

58 St Aldates
Oxford
OX1 1ST
United Kingdom

Publishing Director: Sarah Thorpe
Managing Editor: Tanya Whatling,
Editor: Jane Holt

Cover Illustration: Peter Sutton
Illustrations: Debbie Hinks, Gema Arquero
Recording: Maria Jeanette Christiansen, Mauri Corretjé

Printed in Spain
ISBN: 978-84-668-1592-5
Deposito Legal: M-30404-2012
© Richmond / Santillana Educación S.L., 2012